# The Customer Manifesto

## HOW BUSINESS HAS FAILED CUSTOMERS & WHAT IT TAKES TO EARN LOYALTY

Pamela Herrmann

CreateSpace
NORTH CHARLESTON, SC

CreateSpace
4900 LaCross Road
North Charleston, SC 29406 USA
www.TheCustomerManifesto.com

Cover art:
Lonnie Weis | Elevator | www.elvtr.net

Ordering Information:
Quantity sales. Special discounts are available on quantity purchases by corporations, associations, and others. For details, contact the "Special Sales Department" at the address above.

The Customer Manifesto/ Pamela Herrmann. —1st ed.
ISBN-13: 978-1503035010

# Contents

80% of companies say they deliver "superior" customer service.
Yet only 8% of people think these same companies deliver
"superior" customer service.

—LEE RESOURCES

# Preface

As a successful entrepreneur, inventor, educator, and consultant, I've helped thousands of small business owners grow their profits by identifying the broken links in their work flow, creating an exceptional customer experience, and increasing their traffic. The old adage, "Nothing personal, it's just business," couldn't be farther from the truth in today's economy. Business *is* personal. Leveraging social proof, both through word of mouth marketing and online, begins when a business has developed lasting loyalty from its customers. Lasting loyalty happens when we feel a strong feeling of support or allegiance to someone.

This book summarizes for a general audience results from a query put to customers, **"What would a business have to do in order to earn your loyalty?"** *The Customer Manifesto* is the result of that query. By understanding what customers want to *feel* when they transact with a business, we can quickly adapt the way we interact with them with the goal of growing the relationship to the level of evangelist. An evangelist is someone who will willingly and happily provide critical social proof through business ratings and review websites, and through social networking.

This book provides best practices from the highest-rated businesses in hospitality and insights from enterprise-level businesses that have invested billions of dollars to improve the customer experience. We are bringing these best practices to the small, local business owner so that they can learn how to create an exceptional experience with every transaction.

These stories and lessons are presented in the framework of the retail business, but these principles very much apply to the service-based business where customers may be calling you or an online business where you are measuring and monitoring the customer experience through the lens of your website analytics.

Technology is an amazing tool for growing sales, but it is a waste of the two most valuable resources a small business has -- time and money -- if the customer experience is fair to middling. An exceptional experience is created when we prove to customers that they are valued and appreciated with every action, interaction, reaction and transaction.

There have been many people who have influenced the development of this book, but I owe special gratitude to a few people whom I wish to thank. A very special acknowledgement to Dr. Carrie Rose, Ed.D, whose editorial judgment has helped shape this work. Lonnie Weis, who patiently keeps my ship on course, the sails trimmed and the rudder steady. My children Laura and Elliott, from whom I have learned perhaps as much as they have learned from me.

Denver, November 2014

# [1]

# Introduction

I WAS A FRESHMAN in college the summer I traveled from my home in California to my father's family reunion in Chicago. My dad and I had the opportunity to spend an afternoon in the old German neighborhood on the north side where he was raised.

We strolled down the street of his neighborhood, and he recalled stories of growing up in the post-Depression era: playing baseball with a stick and a worn-out ball, how money was so tight they once had to eat cranberries for two weeks and how his single mother had worked tirelessly to support him and his brothers.

He pointed up to his bedroom window on the second floor of their walk-up apartment on North Barry Street and described how thick the ice was on the inside of the window most winter nights.

When we came to the end of the block, my father suddenly stopped dead in his tracks and stared at the corner bakery store. He quietly said, "Oh my God. That store was there when I was growing up."

We pushed open the door and crossed the threshold and a little bell gently announced our arrival. I'll never forget the look on my father's face as he gazed up at it and smiled; it was the same bell he had heard thousands of times as a child. It was as if a familiar friend were calling his name.

The double doors from the kitchen swung open and out walked a little round woman with gray hair neatly pinned into a bun. She was wiping her hands on her apron and she greeted us with a warm smile.

"Oh my God," was all that my father could whisper.

He recognized her immediately as the bakery owner from when he was a boy. He half-dismissively told her his name and pointed down the street in the direction of his house, thinking there was no possible way she would remember him or his family.

Her mouth dropped open and she put her chubby little hands to her face. I could see her eyes glistening and her head slowly moving from side to side as she stared at him in amazement.

She indeed remembered my father, his brothers and my grandmother. It felt as though I were in a parallel universe as I stood off to the side and watched the two of them catch up.

So it begs the question: How many of your customers will you remember in 30 years and more importantly, how many of them will remember you? What is the imprint your business is leaving?

# [2]

# Offline to Online

OUR BUSINESS CLIMATE has been in a state of transition, particularly over the last five years as Internet marketing strategies and resources are more readily available at an affordable price to the small business owner. Yet when we hold up our smartphone and ask small business owners why their websites aren't mobile-responsive, they mostly shrug their shoulders. They tell us they know they need to be doing certain things online, like social media, but they really don't know enough to make a decision about the investment in online marketing.

*A nondecision for any business owner is the weakest position he can find himself in.*

The lost opportunity costs for a small business who can't be found online is enormous. Having a website that cannot properly be navigated through a mobile device represents one of the biggest gaps for a business today. Seventy-eight percent of mobile searches for a local business result in a transaction. A mobile-responsive website is as critical a tool for a business as a telephone. Small business owners wear many hats, and understanding all the elements of online marketing is a beast. It's changing too quickly for even the most intelligent businessperson to keep up with and takes an enormous amount of time to implement.

# what you need to know

The key areas a business owner needs to have general knowledge in so that she can make decisions about how to market online include:

1. Search Engine Optimization (SEO) -- how to position your business on the path of consumers who are looking for your solution
2. Social media -- how to choose a primary network, attract your ideal customer, and consistently engage with your audience
3. Website elements -- the critical "must haves" on your home page
4. Email marketing -- how to build a list and effectively communicate value with them
5. Videos -- how to get your business at the top of the search queries

The solution is to educate yourself so that you have competency, not mastery. Competency allows you to make investment decisions and manage the outsourcing with the experts. Competency takes you out of nondecision-making mode and allows you to be proactive with your growth strategies.

The most interesting thing about the way the Internet is shaping business is being driven by consumer behavior online. With the powerful consumer review websites like Google+, TripAdvisor and MerchantCircle, consumers are chiming in using a very big bullhorn to tell the world exactly what they think about a particular business.

If you want to stand out online as being the best in your category, you have to be unforgettable for the right reasons. Investing in your customer relationships the way our grandparents did so they feel valued is the gateway to leveraging your reputation online. This is the honey hole for businesses today.

Breaking through and standing out among your competitors is as much about the return to old-school connectedness with your customers as it is about driving traffic from online sources.
Before you utilize a powerful tool like the Internet to amplify your brand message, you first need to provide an exceptional customer experience.

*If you're mediocre at delivering your products or services, your customers are vulnerable to your competitor's offerings.*

Consumers don't go online and rate mediocre businesses. They're either talking about businesses that do it exceptionally well, or really, really poorly. Have you ever given a restaurant a 3-star review? No one has time for that.

*Middle of the road will get you one thing, and that is run over.*

Being exceptional with your customers is what will drive your increased sales and expand your word-of-mouth marketing into the online space where untold numbers of people in your community or beyond will get to know you, like you and trust you.

> *What does it take to make a customer feel loyalty to a business to the degree that they would refer someone?*

What exactly do they want, need or desire? What has to happen consistently with every action, reaction, interaction and transaction?

## reverse-engineer what consumers want

*The Customer Manifesto* will show you how easy it is to create these deeper-level bonds that are the foundation to lasting loyalty so that you can have endless referrals from your happy customers.

The businesses best positioned to succeed in today's economy are doing one thing differently. They are standing out by providing an exceptional customer experience.

So we've studied the best of the best at delivering an exceptional customer experience. These are enterprise-level businesses. We're taking their best practices and we're unpacking them for small, local businesses so they can stand out in a sea of sameness by being the best in their category. You will learn what enterprise-level businesses have spent billions of dollars to understand about their customers. The slight turn of the dial will yield high results in the form of increased sales.

# The Customer Manifesto

We asked customers, "What does a business have to do in order to earn your loyalty?"

... And the most common responses are reflected here:

## 1. "I love when I'm welcomed"

When I walk in the door, or call you on the phone, please greet me warmly as if I'm a returning customer, or a friend you haven't seen in a while.

## 2. Acknowledge me

I'll patiently wait my turn. However, let's be honest, I'm waiting to hand you my money. So look up and acknowledge me by thanking me for my patience and assure me you'll be with me promptly.

## 3. Hear me

What makes me the happiest is when I feel like you're listening to me and understanding me. Even when I don't know exactly how to express what I'm looking for, take the initiative and help connect the dots in my mind.

## 4. Speak my love language

Seduce me with the love language that all customers melt to: "My pleasure," "Absolutely," "You're most welcome" in place of "Sure," "No problem," or "Yeah."

## 5. Exceed my expectations

If you see me pondering, reaching, searching or wandering, it's probably because I'm looking for something I can't find. Anticipate this and show me that you care by guiding me to the solution, instead of telling me where I can find it.

## 6.  Make me feel comfortable

I appreciate an environment that is clean and comfortable, and I notice the little details that you may not see. Look at your business through the eyes of your customer and then you'll see what I'm seeing. Dust, wipe, clean, tidy up, rinse, repeat.

## 7.  Be a Genshai Jedi

Genshai is an ancient Hindi word meaning "never to treat others, or yourself, in a way to make them feel small." Lift those around you; don't make me feel like I'm putting you out.

## 8.  Respect my money

I believe in the flow of energy in money, so instead of handing back my change all at once, kindly count it out.  My money is like gold.

## 9.  Dazzle me

Wow me! The chord of appreciation has been lying dormant within my emotional fabric.

## 10.  Thank me

When you look me in the eye, smile and sincerely thank me for my business, it connects me to you and your brand. The purpose of business is to get and keep customers, so show me sincere appreciation for my business.

# [4]

# "I Love When I'm Welcomed"

*"When I walk in the door or call you on the phone, please greet me warmly as if I'm a returning customer or a friend you haven't seen in a while."*

HOW MANY TIMES have you walked into a store and you either didn't get welcomed or it was pretty flat? You got the sense that it wasn't sincere; it was more of a formality? Perhaps something the employee was expected to do.

The feedback we received from one of the people we queried was, "Hey, you know, when I walk in the door or call you on the phone, please greet me warmly as if I'm a returning customer or a friend that you haven't seen in a while."

*Even if it's the first time someone has walked in the store, they should always be greeted as if they are a long-lost friend.*

I recently visited Cooperstown, N.Y., home of the Baseball Hall of Fame, as my son was playing in a baseball tournament there.

One of the team moms said to me, "You really should go into Stage Coach Coffee. They have the most amazing Mexican Mocha."

So sure enough, the next morning I walked in there and when I got to the front of the line, this gentleman says to me,

"Hi! How are you doing today?"

"Excellent. Thanks!" I replied.

"What can I get for you?"

"Well, everybody is raving about this Mexican Mocha coffee you make," I said. "So make it a medium, please."

"Good choice" he replied. And as he's making my drink, he asks me, "Are you visiting from out of town?"

"I am," I said. "My son's playing in a weeklong baseball tournament."

"Oh, excellent! How are they doing?" he asked.

It is at this very moment that it occurs to me that he's not an employee at this coffee shop. He's acting more vested, more curious than an employee. He must be the owner.

So I asked him, "Is this your business?"

"Yes," he replied. "My brother Chris and I own it. We roast our own beans in the back. You should go check it out. We've got this huge, huge facility back there. My name's Matt, by the way."

"Thanks! Nice to meet you, Matt. I'm Pamela." So he handed the coffee to me and I went off on my merry way.

The next morning I went back to Stagecoach and I got to the front of the line and the same guy asked, "Hey Pam, how's it going today?"

And I'm startled. I'm thinking to myself, and I actually said out loud, "I can't believe you remembered my name!"

"Well, I bet you don't remember my name."

"It's Matt," I replied.

And he repeated back to me, "I can't believe you remember my name!"

He then asked me, "Are you going to have the Mexican Mocha again today?"

I was astounded. "I can't believe you remembered what I had yesterday!"

"Look, I'm a trained professional," he laughed. "And this is what I do" As he whipped it up he asked me how my son did in the tournament yesterday.

When he handed my drink back to me, I told him, "You know, I'm going to go online and review your business since you're doing such a great job."

So, the third day I walk in and I'm standing there in line. There are a few people in front of me. He looks up and he sees me and he says loudly, "Hey Pam, thanks so much for reviewing my business yesterday on TripAdvisor. Tell you what, coffee today is on me." And everyone else in line slowly turns their heads and look at me and then at Matt with eyebrows raised and I kind of shrugged.

Matt did a couple of really important things in that very moment:

- He gave me a big shout-out in front of other customers so they heard that reviews mattered to him.

- He reciprocated my gesture by buying me a cup of coffee, which made me feel good, and it may inspire those who heard our conversation to also provide a review.

By the fourth day he was introducing me to his wife and kids who just happened to pop in for a scone. It made me feel really special, like I was a regular and part of this clan.

Matt really nailed it because he made me feel like the character Norm from "Cheers." Every customer wants to feel like Norm, right? The bar is an extension of his home. He has his own stool and they all shout out his name when he walks in the door. That's how we want to feel. Like we matter and we're valued.

Principle number 3 from *Six Ways to Make People Like You*, as written by Dale Carnegie in the classic *How to Win Friends and Influence People,* is, "Remember that a person's name is to that person the sweetest and most important sound in any language."

# 'hello' to referral

The welcome is the seed that grows into a referral, when tended properly. It sets the tone for how interested the business is in getting to know you. There are six phases that take us from a "hello" to a referral.

Word of Mouth

It begins with the welcome and how we greet someone. From the greeting we can easily move into rapport, which is the basic chitchat. Rapport leads to relationship when we find we have something in common. When you've done a good job of building the relationship, your customer begins to trust you. Then they become loyal to you. It's at this point that they will refer others to you through word-of-mouth marketing.. What Matt did exceptionally well was taking me through this entire process very, very quickly.

*On average, loyal customers are worth about 10X as much as their first purchase.*

So, a key number for your business is the value of the one-time transaction of a customer. This is calculated by doing some simple math. Just take your total daily sales and divide by the number of transactions. For example, if you have 35 transactions and your daily sales are $3,053 the average transaction is about $87. So when you provide an exceptional customer experience, the value of that one transaction is up to 10 times that number. That can come in the form of repeat business or in the form of referrals.

If you are doing really well at building relationships to the degree of loyalty, they will refer others to you and this is where the low-hanging fruit is for your small business.

So what did Matt do? Matt was successful at creating rapport in that first transaction. A relationship developed in the second transaction when he remembered my name and engaged me in conversation about my son. Trust and loyalty came in the third transaction when he talked about introducing me to the new Chamber of Commerce director, and introduced me to his wife and kids.

How many referrals did he receive as a result of our relationship? Well, he received two referrals. One word-of-mouth referral that brought me to his business and then one online referral that I gave. That one will influence countless customers through the lifetime of his business who are looking online for a good coffee shop in Cooperstown.

How much did Matt invest to get these referrals? He invested a little bit of time and effort and probably less than $1 in hard costs by paying for my coffee.

This is the power you can create for your business as well. Everyone who comes to your business is an influencer and, with proper nurturing, everyone has the potential to become your raving fan.

*What is your current practice for making customers feel welcomed?*

Take two or three minutes and reflect on what your current practice is for making customers feel welcomed when they call your business. Or if you have a brick and mortar business, what are you saying to them when they cross the threshold? Or if you have a website, how do you immediately make someone feel welcomed when they land on your homepage?

# it's how you say it that matters

Let's take a page from the Office Depot playbook. Enterprise level corporations like Office Depot spend millions of dollars on customer insights. Insights tell them exactly what it is their customers are doing and what they're thinking. Based on those insights they make adaptations to the way their employees deliver these products and services. By making one small change in the way they greeted their customer, Office Depot created a massive increase in their sales.

The greeting went from, "Welcome to Office Depot. Thanks for coming in," to "What brings you to Office Depot today?" while simultaneously handing the customer a basket.

It seems like just a nuance, doesn't it? What they learned is that their customers are coming in for a specific reason. There is a very clear intention coming through the door. They are not walking into Office Depot to browse; customers go to Nordstrom to browse.

So the combination of what they're saying and what they're doing is the difference. The employees are making the assumption that they *will* help you find the thing you are coming in for, that you *will* put that thing in your basket and that you *will* walk out with a purchase.

This one tweak in their greeting resulted in a 40 percent increase in customers who bought something before leaving the store. If you have 10 customers in a day who walk out of your store or leave your website without buying anything, imagine what it could do to your daily sales, your monthly sales, quarterly sales, annual sales, compounded for the lifetime of your business if four of the 10 of those people transacted. It would have a huge, huge impact on a small business' bottom line.

## 'loyalty' loosely defined

Now that you see why it's important to master the greeting, let's take a look at a business that didn't quite hit the nail on the head. A customer we surveyed named Suzie told us this story. She said her son has a pet lizard. (I don't know, something about pet and lizard in one sentence is an interesting notion. I tend to think if you can't cuddle it, is it really a pet? Anyway, that's a debate over a beer.) Back to Suzie's story:

On a weekly basis Suzie goes into PetSmart to buy live crickets for her son's lizard. Live crickets cost 11 to 14 cents each. Suzie drives past PetSmart's big-box competitor, Petco, in order to get her crickets for a few cents less. Suzie is in PetSmart every single week and invariably it's the same gal working behind the cash register.

> "The cashier never says hello, she just asks this question, 'Are you a member of our loyalty program?' "

Suzie said she smiles and nods her head. She said, "Gosh, you know, I've been going there for over a year, every single week. This gal should recognize me." The cashier has been trained to ask this question about loyalty, and she does a great job of consistently asking it however disinterested or unenthusiastic it may be, but the irony is that the relationship isn't about loyalty at all.

So Suzie gives her phone number and everything the cashier needs to take this transaction to the next level and make Suzie feel special is right there on the computer screen -- her name! The missed opportunity is that she never does.

She never looks at the screen and says, "Hey Suzie, great to see you again. How's it going today? How's the lizard doing?" The cashier does nothing to engage her.

# the Main Street advantage

Being excellent is highly profitable. Seven out of 10 customers said they are willing to spend more with companies that provide an excellent customer experience. So if you want to differentiate yourself and stand out, this is the way to do it. You really have to be excellent at engagement and make people feel special. Consumers are telling us this is what they want.

What do we need to do to make someone feel welcome? There are five components to making someone feel welcome and these are soft skills anyone can learn.

Making Someone Feel Welcome

| 1 | 2 | 3 | 4 | 5 |
|---|---|---|---|---|
| What To Say | How To Say It | Body Language | Be Curious | Anticipate Needs |

Customers are deciding very quickly:

- Do they like you?
- Do they trust you?
- Are you like them? In other words, do you share the same values?
- Are you authentic?

# what to say

Are your customers coming in to browse or with a purpose? This goes back to our example with Office Depot. Determine why your customers are coming in and how can you modify your greeting to match their intentions.

# how to say it

Did you know that at Disney they train all their employees to smile when they answer the phone? Why? Because we can actually hear when someone is smiling and it automatically elevates the mood in the conversation. Besides, customers spend more money when they're happy.

# body language

Act eager to help. Have you ever been in a store browsing and the employee's body language doesn't convey anticipating the customer needs? How did they look in that moment? Were they slouched over? Were they standing behind the counter? Were they facing in the opposite direction? What was their body doing that was conveying to you the feeling of disinterest? Take stock of how your employees are representing your business through the use of body language.

# be curious

When I mastered how to be authentically curious my ability to construct a conversation with the goal of converting sales went up exponentially because I was connecting with people very quickly in understanding:

- What is going on with them today?
- Where would they rather be? In other words, what solution do they want?
- What is the biggest challenge in getting that solution? In other words, what do they think are the obstacles between where they are and where they want to be?
- What are they willing to do to get that challenge taken off their path?

This is a powerful four-step process, especially if you're a service provider, because it will help you paint the picture for the customer as to how your solution dovetails with the result they want. The big trust builder in this process is that if you don't have the solution your customer is looking for, offer to connect them with someone who does have that solution. It builds trust because the customer now sees that your priority is in them getting the appropriate solution not you making a sale.

They trust you immediately when you say to them, "You know what, I want to help you but I know someone that is a better fit for what you want. Let me connect you with them."

In other words: give it away. Let them go and I guarantee you they will come back in the form of referrals. I have seen this over and over. It is highly effective at building trust. There is some universal truth to the abundance that Steven Covey references in his book, *The 7 Habits of Highly Successful People* that this conveys. "Live in that space of abundance. Let's aim to get the customer the thing that they want."

# anticipating your customers' needs

Here's a great example from my business partner, Dr. Carrie Rose, Ed.D. She was at a place called Extract Juice Bar in Winter Park, Fla. She ordered a juice, asked where the restroom was and mentioned that she would need to use her laptop when she returned. The owner, Stacy Davis, walked her down the hallway because the restroom was in a counterintuitive location and she didn't want Carrie to get lost.

When Carrie returned, her juice was ready, and Stacy said, "I thought you'd need this so you can hop onto the Internet" and she handed her a sticky note with their Wi-Fi password written down on it.

This is what anticipating the needs of a customer looks like. See how little tiny things that seem inconsequential actually have a lot of meaning? Carrie was so impressed with the overall customer experience that she tweeted about this business, did a review on Yelp and posted about the experience on Facebook. That is the power that a high-touch welcome has for quickly moving a customer through the continuum of relationship building that leads to a review online.

The way in which you welcome customers to your business has an enormous affect on your sales. It will:

- Increase your customer satisfaction
- Increase the number of referrals
- Differentiate you from your competition
- Keep you 'top of mind.'

# [5]

# "Acknowledge Me"

*" I'll patiently wait my turn. However, let's be honest, I'm waiting to hand you my money. So look up and acknowledge me by thanking me for my patience, and assure me that you'll be with me promptly."*

**CAUTION: INCOMING RANT.** The fact that a customer felt that this basic concept needed to be stated is a direct indication of how low the customer experience has fallen. There is no justification for a customer to ever feel like he is not being acknowledged. This is business 101.

The purpose of business is two-fold: To get customers and to keep customers. They're walking into a business, ready to hand over their hard-earned money, and they feel like they're not even being acknowledged.

## core values are tied to profits

My son Elliott and I ate at a quick-service restaurant called Smashburger recently. They are a fast-growing burger chain with over 200 restaurants worldwide. It was perfection from the moment we walked in until the moment we walked out. What did they do?

There was a customer at the register and the cashier looked up at us, smiled, said hello and told us she'd be with us right away. She had a nice expression on her face, very patient and kind. On the table tent there was a card with the back-story of the small ranchers in Colorado who provided the 100 percent Angus meat and their core values around animal care for food production. As I read this, I learned about the character of the business because I'm one of those consumers who wonder where my beef comes from. Is it from a cow in one of those sad feedlots or is it from a happy cow in a green meadow?. Two employees brought our food out and asked us if there was anything else they could do for us.

A few minutes later, the manager came over and gave us (yes, gave us) a serving of their awesome rosemary and olive oil fries so we could try them out. This was a nice touch everyone loves to be given little gifts and it cost them a few pennies.

A little bit later the manager was wiping down tables and checked in with us again. When we got up to leave, the manager, who was at the other end of the restaurant, gave us a big shout-out of thanks for coming in.

Here is what I would guess are Smashburger's core values:

- That every customer is treated as a valued guest
- To express gratitude by being nice
- That cleanliness creates comfort
- To provide the highest-quality burger
- To show gratitude to every customer.

*3 in 5 Americans would try a new brand or company for a better service experience.*

Source: American Express Survey, 2011

Here is a stone-cold fact: Smashburger can't afford to perform below this level because there is too much at stake. We'll go elsewhere. There is a lot of competition in the quick-service restaurant sector.

# the upside of culture

Let's take a closer look at some empirical evidence that shows the relationship between company culture and sales growth. In a Forbes Magazine article, *Does Corporate Culture Drive Financial Performance? 2/10/2011, a* comparison between 12 firms that had performance-enhancing culture vs. 20 firms that did not, the results are staggering. In all data points, the companies with performance-enhancing cultures outperform. The strength of a company's corporate culture influences its increase in equity value, as evidenced by the 900 percent increase in equity value of these 12 companies.

## Company Culture Has A Direct Effect On Sales Growth

■ Companies With Performance Enhancing Cultures

■ Companies Without Performance Enhancing Cultures

# the low-hanging fruit

Growing your profits is ridiculously simple, and for a small business it is a relatively low-cost investment with huge return on investment (ROI). And the fact of the matter is customers can detect on some level within minutes of walking into a store what the core values of the business owner are, even when you're not present. Your employees are mirroring your values positively or negatively. In the world of Main Street businesses this is the true definition of " trickle down" economics.

As the leader you have to take 100 percent of the responsibility for the customer experience. You are the determining factor in whether or not a customer-service orientation in place. You are the determining factor in whether or not your staff has been trained to extend those values. You are the determining factor in whether or not your customers *feel* those values within minutes of walking into your store. End of story.

> *80% of companies say they deliver "superior" customer service. Yet only 8% of people think these same companies deliver "superior" customer service.*
>
> *—LEE RESOURCES*

# don't drink the Kool-Aid

Maybe you are thinking you're doing a great job with your customers. Maybe you are and you're one of the 8 percent who are delivering an exceptional customer experience. No judgment here, but it doesn't matter how YOU think you're doing. What matters is what your customers think. Only 4 percent of unhappy customers voice their complaints and 78 percent are abandoning their transaction because of poor service. So there is a massive disconnect between how well companies think they're doing and what the customers are telling us. We see this all the time -- business owners who are resistant to even the remotest possibility that there could be a way to improve. Being open to and committing to change takes courage. Trusting your employees takes courage. The most courageous decision about your business is behind you. It happened when you decided to open your business. **Now it's a matter of how you committed you are so** that you are always relevant.

# being relevant

As a small business owner you don't have the resources to hire consultants to analyze what your customers think about you like the enterprise-level businesses do. The bottom-line question is,

ARE YOU WILLING TO CONTINUALLY STRIVE TO IMPROVE SO THAT YOU ARE ALWAYS THE BEST IN YOUR CATEGORY?

If you are like most small businesses you have fewer than five employees and you may not be involved in every single interaction with your customers. If you want to see sales growth, it is imperative that you and your employees are communicating your core values. What's at stake is your brand reputation. That means every employee needs to deliver your products and services at the highest level, every single time.

What are your business's core values and how do you currently ensure that they are being perceived at every level of your business? If you are thinking, "I don't know, I've never asked myself this before," it's OK.

This is easy to create and the benefits are huge. It will change the way you feel about your business. It will excite your employees. Most importantly, your customers will notice it and will align with your values, become loyal to your business and ultimately drive increased profits.

There are key points that we can take from enterprise-level businesses that have incorporated core values into their culture. Once you are clear on the core values of your company you are able to excel on many levels.

Core values provide a set of guidelines that help your staff make critical decisions that affect the customer. They will make decisions based on an agreed-upon set of guidelines dictated by the company values. Without these guidelines, there is no fence around the decision-making process. When your people are in alignment with the core values, every thought, word and deed revolves around exceptional delivery.

When you hire people who share similar core values they will automatically resonate with the culture, and they will naturally have the behaviors, attitudes and actions that ultimately drive congruent results.

There is a perception that developing core values is a waste of time that the values will wind up just like your mission statement; hung up on the wall or emblazoned on your website. Just like anything in life, it's only an idea until you do something with it. Unfortunately, many organizations define company values by what leaders think the values should be. This top-down, leader-directed approach doesn't connect or motivate people based on what matters to them. Instead of identifying values at the top and passing them down to your staff, an approach that elicits and reflects the deepest values of the company are designed by the employees who deliver the core values. This will serve the most important person in the equation: The customer.

When employees have ownership in the creation of the core values, they will inherently use them to drive the company culture, strategy and activities. They become highly productive and enjoy where they work. More importantly, if you do it in this way, your frontline employees will communicate them to your customers in every action, interaction, reaction and transaction. This is what builds loyalty to a brand.

What are core values? They are a set of dictums that are very loose in nature, somewhat subjective and open to individual interpretation, but ultimately reflect what matters most to the organization.

# attitudes matter

A customer named Paul shared with us a transaction he had at a Pep Boys automotive supply store that illustrated to him his value in the eyes of the employees. After waiting 10 minutes in a long line, it was finally his turn. The overworked employee leaned on the service counter with both elbows, looked at a computer screen, and said in an obligatory way, "How can I try and help you." No greeting was offered. No thank you was extended for the patience needed to wait.

Paul was annoyed so (being a Star Wars buff) he channeled his inner Yoda and replied, "Do or do not, there is no try." He now drives 10 miles out of his way and pays more to a smaller independent business out of spite for the poor service he received. Customers like Paul are voting with their wallet, and they're also voting online.

> *7 out of 10 customers said they were willing to spend more with companies that provide an excellent customer experience.*
>
> *Source: American Express Survey, 2011*

What do you think are the core values of this company based on what was projected by this employee? What do you think are the core values of the manager? What do you think are the core values of this employee? As you can see, it is very difficult to clearly define whose values were being projected in that example; that of the employee, that of the manager or that of the corporation. The bottom line is that it doesn't really matter. All that matters is how Paul *feels* about how he was treated.

> *"Although your customers won't love you if you give bad service, your competitors will."*
>
> - *Kate Zabriskie, Founder, Business Training Works*

Here are examples of enterprise-level businesses with clearly defined core values that are effectively incorporated into their culture.

## Zappos Core Values

- Deliver WOW through service
- Embrace and drive change
- Create fun and a little weirdness
- Be adventurous, creative and open-minded
- Create fun and a little weirdness
- Be adventurous, creative, and open-minded
- Pursue growth and learning
- Build open and honest relationships with communication
- Build a positive team and family spirit
- Do more with less
- Be passionate and determined
- Integrate the core values into everything you do.

## Google's Core Values

- Focus on the user and all else will follow
- It's best to do one thing really, really well
- Fast is better than slow

- Democracy on the web works
- You don't need to be at your desk to need an answer
- You can make money without doing evil
- There's always more information out there
- The need for information crosses all borders
- You can be serious without a suit
- Great just isn't good enough.

Your bottom-line profits are tied to your company's core values and they are translated directly to the employee from you. From the employee they translate to the customer and within moments, the customer is deciding whether you share their values. If your core values are well established and embraced by your employees, you will never have to wonder if your customers are being acknowledged.

> *When people believe they share values with a company, they will remain loyal to that brand.*
>
> *Howard Schultz, CEO, Starbucks*

# [6]

# "Hear Me"

*"What makes me the happiest is when I feel like you're listening to me and understanding me. Even when I don't know exactly how to express what I'm looking for, take the initiative and help connect the dots in my mind."*

THE ASSET VALUE of listening goes up when there is scarcity in the marketplace. This is the way you differentiate yourself personally and in your business. Why? Because few people are actually doing it.

At a primal level we are geared for personal interactions that are rooted in a balance of speaking and listening. With technology here to stay and everything around us moving at warp speed, the only thing that won't change is our need for shared and equitable dialogue. What's interesting is that your equity goes up with others when you are interested in what they are saying and when you're connecting to their words. Think of a real conversation as two pieces of a puzzle that fit together to create a whole picture.

Two individual pieces are more than the sum of their parts when they are engaged in a cohesive interaction.

Connecting at a deeper level and shifting into highly effective trust building is in direct proportion to your skill level of listening and will take an ordinary conversation and make it extraordinary.

## The benefits of listening:

- Develops loyalty
- Demonstrates respect
- Quickly takes the conversation from rapport to relationship
- Unique and rare in today's business climate
- Lays the foundation for the future sale
- Creates massive momentum
- Is disarming
- Helps people feel valued
- Creates a two-way engagement
- People feel understood
- Creates raving fans that convert to referrals.

When we talk about the art and science of listening, it's important to first understand what happens when we're not effective at listening. We are ineffective at listening when:

- We react instead of respond
- We misunderstand
- We misinterpret what we think we're hearing and filter it through our world view as opposed to the intention of the speaker
- We argue
- We interrupt.

Barriers to effective listening:

- Exhibiting bias or prejudice
- Language differences or accents
- Distractions, like noises in the room, text messages, phone calls, other people or nearby activities
- Worry, fear or anger
- Lack of attention span. Don't let your mind wander.
- Interrupting to make your own point or share your own personal experiences
- Finishing people's sentences
- Quick-draw responses
- Giving unsolicited advice
- Fidgeting, shifting your body weight often and looking at your watch.

# the art of woo

In order to have a deeper-level understanding you have to be engaged, present in the conversation and an active listener. It takes a lot of concentration and dogged determination to actively listen. Most of us are in the habit of thinking, processing and preparing for a reaction before we have fully understood what the speaker is saying. The little wheels in our heads are always turning, buzzing and whirring.

If we are only waiting until it is our turn to speak, it makes the person we are with feel not so special, as if you have something better to do or somewhere else you would rather be. If you're looking to woo a prospect, the best way to do that is by being fully present in the conversation and listening intently in order to understand.

When you have polished and honed this skill, the benefits personally, professionally and financially will far exceed your expectations. Those around you will sense your caring nature and will quickly feel at ease. You will find people are comfortable telling you things they have never told anyone. They trust you. You'll feel your ability to connect with just about anyone growing. This is a very authentic way to do business because ultimately you will have access to important information, therefore helping you provide the right solution.

The value of being present in conversations transcends business. The greatest benefit will come in your personal relationships. You'll find you are parenting with greater patience and your ability to relate to your family and friends is strengthened. All the relationships in your life will be enriched.

We listen by focusing on being in the now, being present. How do we focus on being present?

- Give the speaker your undivided attention and acknowledge the message. Recognize that nonverbal communication also "speaks" loudly
- Look at them directly
- Put aside distracting thoughts
- Don't mentally prepare a rebuttal
- Avoid being distracted by environmental factors
- "Listen" to the speaker's body language
- Refrain from side conversations when listening in a group setting.

# kicking it grandpa style

Next time you have a conversation with someone, I'd like you to visualize a grandpa. He is a sweet, gentle soul sitting on the front porch of his home gently rocking in his rocking chair. He's sipping his tall glass of lemonade, telling you a story and just taking life nice and slow.

Now as you're having this conversation, I'd like to invite you to kick it grandpa style and just slow it down. The words you hear, just let them hang there, kind of like a cartoon bubble. Don't jump to finish their sentence, don't interrupt, just let the meaning of the message come through. Ask questions that clarify what they just said. Ask it in a way that says you're curious about more. "Tell me more." "Why do you think that is?"

This is a bit painful at first because you will find the conversations to be rather one-sided. People are desperately wanting someone to listen to them, so be that person. With discipline and a little practice you will soon find people telling you things they've never told anyone. They will tell you you're the most interesting person they've talked to in a long time, even though they've done all the talking.

## We listen by being interested

How do we build deeper-level rapport? It starts with the mastery of listening. When we come across good listeners in business or socially, it often takes us by surprise. An individual who is a good listener projects herself as interesting when in reality, she is just being interested. So the individual in the conversation feels listened to and heard with no idea that he knows little about the other person.

Tony Hsieh, CEO of Zappos, has cultivating good listening as one of the core values of his company. While you may not typically think of listening skills when you consider the qualities of an action-oriented leader, you should. The art of listening helps them learn what they need to know about the world around them. Hsieh asked all his employees to share their personal values so he could incorporate them into the company's values and culture. There is a cultural perspective interwoven into the process of developing relationships.

## We listen by being intentional

There are countless challenges that can arise in a conversation when we are not in active listening mode, including:

- Losing your ability to effectively influence, persuade and negotiate
- Conflict and arguments can arise
- Misunderstandings
- You move into judgment and view their words through your worldview
- You become too wrapped up in thinking about your response before their thought has been expressed
- You react instead of respond
- People feel used or ignored as if their words don't matter

## Interruptions

By becoming a better listener, your ability to influence, persuade and negotiate with others is heightened. What's more, you'll avoid conflict and misunderstandings. All this is necessary for workplace success. So how do you demonstrate you are listening intentionally?

- Be without judgment. People who speak from their perspective come from a place of "This is the best I know how." It doesn't matter what they're talking about, this is their mindset. So if we know and have the perception that this is where they are, it is a powerful place to start engaging without reacting and that's what helps us to connect at a heart level.
- Be deliberate with your listening and remind yourself frequently that your goal is to truly hear what the other person is saying. Set aside all other thoughts and behaviors and concentrate on the message.
- Paraphrase to ensure you understand the message. If you don't, then you'll find that what someone says to you and what you hear can be amazingly different.

## We listen by being objective

If you find yourself responding emotionally to what someone has said, say so and ask for more information: "I may not be understanding you correctly, and I find myself taking what you said personally. What I thought you just said is XXX; is that what you meant?"

## 9 Things You can Do To Be A Better Listener:

1. Maintain eye contact with the person talking
2. Keep focused on how they are feeling

3. Show confidence
4. Focus on the content, not the delivery
5. Listen to the message, not the messenger
6. Avoid emotional reactions
7. Pay attention
8. Don't go on a mental vacation, i.e., looking at your phone
9. Treat listening as a challenging mental task.

You can hear without listening. Concentrate on what's being said so you can process it as you hear it. Effective listening skills fuel our social, emotional and professional lives. Listening is a skill, and skills can be developed. Although this is one that may not come naturally, with a bit of consistent practice you will move into high trust.

# [7]

# "Speak My Love Language"

*"Seduce me with the love language that all customers melt to: "My pleasure," "Absolutely," "You're most welcome" in place of "Sure," "No problem," or "Yeah."*

THE MANDARIN ORIENTAL, Las Vegas is one of the leading hotels in North America-. In the words of Richard Baker, executive vice president, "Those awards can be taken away in a moment. It's one thing to earn them, it's a terrible thing to ever lose them."

There is a top-down understanding at the Mandarin of the enormous value that these awards bring to their hotel. This understanding of value is driven by the expectation of their guests and how they are to be treated consistently by the staff.

Mandarin's valet, Glenn Gaffin, loves his work and he exudes pride in what he is delivering to guests. "The answer is 'yes'. Now, what's the question?" Gaffin aspires to make everyone who crosses the threshold of their hotel feel like they're being welcomed home. He understands that he is a cog in a finely tuned engine and if even one failed experience happens, there is much at stake for the brand.

# consumers wield a mighty sword

When we talk about meeting customers' expectations through the language of service, our end goal is to create an experience where they feel welcomed. If the goal is unmet, consumers are not holding back and will go online and share their experiences with others, thereby influencing the purchasing behaviors of untold numbers of consumers who are deciding if they want to do business with you.

> *"The rise of the citizen review site is a sobering development. No longer are you on top of the mountain blasting your marketing message down to the masses through your megaphone. All of a sudden, the masses are conversing with one another. If your service or product isn't any good, they'll out you."*
>
> *- David Pogue, Scientific American*

With the advent of consumer rating websites, like Google+ and TripAdvisor, the power has shifted. It's open kimono time and every business today is totally exposed. Customers are rating their experiences with stars and offering reviews of the wins and epic fails. Those businesses that have the courage to monitor their reputation (and every business committed to improving the way they do business should) has unfettered, unfiltered and unadulterated access to their customers' insights.

The tone and language with which we respond to our customers online is as critically important as what we say and how we say it offline. Every business should have a clearly defined "voice" that represents the brand, and that voice should reflect the core values of the company so there is consistency in every interaction, regardless of the employee.

There is much opportunity for businesses to elevate their staff trainings in the love language of customers. I can't count the number of times I say thank you first to a cashier, when I should be the one being thanked. Without purchases they would cease to exist.

The current accepted language of service lacks intention. Companies have taken their foot off the gas when it comes to educating their employees on the value of high engagement using service language. In the absence of training, your staff will resort to the language they know best and it's generally ineffective. But herein lies the opportunity. Because consumers have such low expectations, it's quite easy to stand out for being exceptional.

At my local grocery store, I asked the service desk employee if I could have a customer comment card. His reply was, "I don't know if we have one. I've never been asked for one so I don't know where it is. I know you can go online and fill out a survey."

Do you see that the language is heavy on the negative side? "I don't know if ..." I've never ..." "I don't know where ..."

What would Glenn Gaffin say?

What customers deserve is nothing short of a can-do response like, "Yes, absolutely, your feedback is important to us. One moment please." Then call the manager and either ask where the cards are or have him come to the front to meet the customer.

The goal is to have your employees consistently and authentically respond in this manner without even thinking about it.

# the art of improvisation

One of the things jazz great Miles Davis was most famous for was his improvisation. Some of his most remarkable recordings were done in one take and couldn't be recreated. Improvisation is the creative activity of immediate ("in the moment") musical composition, which combines performance with communication of emotions and instrumental technique, as well as spontaneous response to other musicians.

So as we train our employees to be great at improvisational conversation, we begin by educating them on the language of your company's culture. Regardless of whether your business is a 5-star world-class hotel or you sell surfboards on the beach, customers appreciate being spoken to in a way that honors them.

You want to hire people who are creative with their people skills so that they deliver that one perfect take, consistently, with every single customer.

> *"Screen for aptitude, hire for attitude."*
>
> *Dave Barger, CEO, JetBlue*

Becoming great at improvisation begins when you become an observer. As you move throughout your day as a consumer, be aware of the language being used with you. What do you like to hear? More importantly, how does it make you feel? Capture these moments and with your staff design the language that best reflects your company culture.

For quick-service restaurants, where inconsistent, impersonal and uninspired interaction with customers reigns supreme, Chick-fil-A stands out as different. Its staff focuses on being quick and personal. For the past two years the Atlanta-based chain was named "best drive-through in America" by the quick-service restaurant trade journal QSR. Why do they stand out?

President and Chief Operating Officer Dan Cathy infuses everyone from franchise owner-operators to teenagers earning $9 an hour with his passion for service and his conviction in its intrinsic worth to the individual as well as the company. Its intrinsic worth to the individual comes in the form of a life skill.

I still recall vividly my first lesson in service language as a 16-year-old cashier at McDonald's. My manager taught me that, "How can I help you?" wasn't the question. The customer knows you are capable of helping them. The question is, "How *may* I help you?" It suggests that you want to and are willing to serve. Big difference.

At the end of each transaction at Chick-fil-A, you don't hear, "You're welcome," "Glad to help," or "Come back and see us." You will hear these two words: "My pleasure." It's distinctive, it's the sort of language you would expect at a 5-star establishment, like the Ritz-Carlton, and besides, it's what Grandpa would say.

# no problem? no bueno!

Recently a customer we surveyed, Bob, was in the tony Cherry Creek neighborhood of Denver at a restaurant called North. When Bob asked the 20-something server about the house wine, she replied, "It's not bad; no one has ever complained about it." After that ringing endorsement Bob decided to go with Grey Goose and soda to which she replied, "No problem."

"No problem" is generational language that has bled into service language. I have noticed this response on the rise with customer-facing employees. I wanted to understand what that expression meant to them. What I learned is that when they say "no problem," what they mean is "sure." They were surprised to learn through this question that "no problem" tells to a customer subliminally that you're doing them a favor. When we ask our kids to take out the garbage, "no problem" is an appropriate response. When we ask our friends if they could possibly bring our child home from practice, "no problem" is an appropriate response.

Every server at a restaurant is a brand ambassador. They are tasked with much more than just moving food and drink from point A to point B. Monkeys and robots can do that (and I think they do in some countries). Our expectation as consumers is that customer-facing staff will know their product offerings, make recommendations, up-sell and ensure that customers like Bob feel like a king when they leave. That is what will inspire him to spread the good word about your business.

# consumers can smell mediocrity

"Meh" is not a sustainable attitude. Regardless of what your business' products or services are, your employees are tasked with always being in the mode of getting and keeping customers.

## What does that sound like?

- "My pleasure"
- "Certainly"
- "Absolutely"
- "You are most welcome."

*"All employees will know the needs of their internal and external customers (guests and employees) so that we may deliver the products and services they expect."*

*From the pages of the Ritz-Carlton playbook*

Your staff should be trained in first-response phrases to commonly asked questions and objections and situations that commonly arise.

If there is a question your staff doesn't know the answer to, the response should be, "That's a great question, let me check with someone and I'll be right back. May I put you on hold?" [Or if they are face to face, "Do you mind if I step away for a moment?"] Then quickly find the person who has the answer. More examples from the Ritz-Carlton:

- "Smile -- We are on stage." Always maintain positive eye contact with our guests. (Use words like- "Good morning," "Certainly," "I will be happy to" and "My pleasure").
- Use proper telephone etiquette. Answer within three rings and with a "smile." When necessary, ask the caller, "May I place you on hold?" Do not screen calls. Eliminate call transfers when possible.

# how are you being represented?

We have a natural need as humans to feel engaged and connected and that's the point from where your brand should start. It doesn't matter what you sell. People want to have a sense of community, a sense of belonging and a sense of engagement.

When customers see a positive culture behind the counter of a business, on the phone or on a website, they want to stay longer and enjoy it because they see a reflection of a positive environment. That begins with your customer-facing employees.

The golden rule is so simple and applicable to all businesses. The key is to hire people who are inherently friendly and who will, by natural extension of their personality, treat your customers in a friendly way with an attitude of service, with the critical thinking skills of an improvisationalist. So it's not just what they're saying, it's the manner in which they're saying it.

Each transaction is unique and can't be typified nor can it be recreated. It's got to be personal and in the moment. It's astounding how effective it is when we link to someone through a simple question. Hire amazing people and let them be themselves because the more they are themselves, the more the customer feels comfortable.

# [8]

# "Exceed My Expectations"

*"If you see me pondering, reaching, searching or wandering, it's probably because I'm looking for something that I can't find. Anticipate this and show me that you care by guiding me to the solution, instead of telling me where I can find it."*

DEARLY BELOVED, we are gathered here today to pay final tribute of respect to the term "Customer Service." Let me offer you the comfort afforded by a newer, fresher, more appropriate term, "Customer Experience."

Customer Service
what we do **to** someone

Customer Experience
what we do **for** someone

In order to exceed expectations, you must transition from "service" to "experience." So what is the difference? The definition of customer service is what we do *to* someone. The customer experience is what we do *for* someone. A customer experience is marked by:

- A warm greeting upon entering
- An inquiry as to what brings us in
- Assistance to the location within their store that has our solution
- Curiosity that helps the employee determines the best solution
- An air of anticipation
- Knowledge of the solution
- The offer of additional assistance
- The acknowledgement of thanks as we're waiting in line
- A warm greeting by the cashier
- The courtesy of counting back our change
- Addressing us by name, when possible
- Eye contact while extending a sincere thank you for our business.

# give 'em the pickle!

Bob Farrell, of Farrell's Ice Cream Parlor based in Portland, Ore. tells the story of a letter he received from a longtime customer. The customer loved the burgers, loved the atmosphere and he especially loved the pickles. He loved them so much that he always asked for a side of them every time he came in. During a visit, the server told him the side of pickles would cost him an additional 75 cents. The customer was so insulted that he wrote to tell Bob telling him that he just lost a customer over 75 cents because he would never come to his restaurant again.

Mr. Farrell was really upset by this letter. He pulled out all the stops and successfully recovered the customer by sending him a handwritten letter and a coupon and the promise that no customer ever would be charged for a side of pickles. He then called together his staff and shared the bigger-picture lesson of customer retention with them. He emphatically stated to them that it boils down to one concept. Give the customer what they want in order to make them happy. In other words, "Give 'em the pickle!!"

Every business should have their equivalent of the pickle; that unexpected extra thing you do that makes you stand out. It's important because it embodies the nature of what an exceptional customer experience is all about: the details and random acts of kindness that help customers walk away happy with your product or service. Whether it is walking with your customer to that thing in the store instead of telling them where it is located, or anticipating their needs by asking, "Another thing you may want to consider ..." Perhaps it's sending a gift card to your clients as thanks for a referral.

## the Main Street advantage

My mother is a very talented floral designer. She used to own a brick and mortar business just east of San Francisco in a town called Lafayette. One of the most powerful things she did was to create a process for a pre-emptive strike to not just avoid complaints, but to build a loyal fan base. At the end of each day an employee would make outbound calls to every customer who received an arrangement. The phone call would go something like this, "We just wanted to make sure that you received your flowers in good order and we wanted to see if you had any questions about how to care for them so that they last as long as possible." This accomplished numerous loyalty objectives:

- If the recipient was dissatisfied in any way, the arrangement was immediately replaced with one that was to their specific liking, even if it meant the new arrangement was delivered at 9 p.m.
- The recipient of the flowers, who was not actually her paying customer, learned about her business and the quality of care they would receive if they were to do business with her.
- On a daily basis, she would resurrect the sales orders from one year prior and for those orders that celebrated an annual event like an anniversary or birthday, the paying customer received a phone call as a reminder that the event was coming up, that her business provided flowers last year and could they be of service again this year. This was her "pickle."
- She demonstrated to the paying customer that their money was well spent with her. The 360-degree customer satisfaction was my mother's number one priority.
- This differentiated her from her competition.
- It exceeded her customers' expectations because it was from the heart and totally unexpected.
- It kept her top of mind.

Do you think 1-800-FLOWERS is able to provide this level of care? No, they're not that agile. Main Street businesses have the ability to steer the ship around the icebergs, make quick decisions, respond appropriately and get the solution in the hands of the customer faster.

## reciprocity rules

The value of a testimonial to a business is enormous in terms of social proof. What makes a lasting impression with your customers is when you reciprocate their gift to your business with a gift in return. The act of gift giving is the mother lode in terms of loyalty building. A simple handwritten card with a $5 gift card for a cup of coffee or a discount on a future purchase is an inexpensive yet high-yielding gesture because, again, it's unexpected.

## every customer is an influencer

I'm always on the watch for how businesses react when something doesn't go as planned. I was visiting my daughter Laura at college and she booked a room near her campus in Chicago through the phone app Airbnb. It was our first time using their service, which connects travelers with private homes. Upon arrival and seeing the place, well, let's just say that it qualified as indoor camping. We decided it wasn't the level of comfort we like and scrambled to find a hotel room at 8:30 p.m. Airbnb's initial email response was a beautifully worded note of apology for our inconvenience and the offer to pay the difference between our room rate and what we paid for the hotel. Nice touch!

But then the next day we received this message, which qualified as an exceptional recovery effort *and* it far exceeded our expectations:

---

**Airbnb Customer Experience**

**Katerina K, Oct 22 11:09:**

Hello Laura,

Thank you so much for taking the additional step to add a payout method.

I know we have promised to reimburse you the difference you had to pay for your hotel stay however we have decided to reimburse you the full amount of $160 USD for your hotel booking. You can see it in your Transaction History > Future Transactions here: https://www.airbnb.com/users/transaction_history/

I hope you also take the opportunity and use the travel coupon of $50 USD for your next trip with Airbnb and we are confident will exceed your expectations.

Kindly,

Katerina K
www.airbnb.com/help

TO RESPOND TO THIS TICKET, REPLY TO THIS EMAIL

---

For them to invest $210 to recover a first-time customer is exceptional indeed. They even point it out at the bottom of the letter what their goal is: "*... we are confident will exceed your expectations.*"

When I relayed this story on Facebook, it was met by responses from many people who had great experiences with Airbnb. Keep in mind, my Klout Score is high (this is a ranking of my influence in the social networks) and for businesses that track such things, they know to pull out all the stops with online influencers. We all have social equity, and it's monitored by smart enterprise-level businesses so that they respond accordingly to a DEFCON 1 situation and avoid nuclear damage to their reputation.

Your customers have influence too, so understand the power and leverage of it by exceeding their expectations every time. It is particularly easy to do right now because consumer expectations are dismally low. The advantage is that by making a few minor adjustments you can wake your customers up from their long hibernation and demonstrate to them that they deserve to be treated well. That they are worthy of being treated well. That they play a very important role in your business and that you are grateful for them.

# [9]

# "Make Me Feel Comfortable"

> *"I appreciate an environment that is clean and comfortable, and I notice the little details that you may not see. Look at your business through the eyes of your customer and then you'll see what I'm seeing. Dust, wipe, clean, tidy up, rinse, repeat.*

Comfort means different things to different people but at a base level making someone comfortable is rooted in creating a relaxed state. For many consumers, being in a relaxed state in a place of business is tied to the cleanliness of the establishment. And nowhere is that more obvious than in a place where you're eating or sleeping.

According to a recent retail consumer study performed by M/A/R/C Research and National In-Store, 14 percent of consumers polled said they would stop visiting a store that was not as clean as they would like. Moreover, 29 percent said they would continue visiting an unclean store only if it was absolutely necessary. While this study focused on a wide range of retail establishments, the quick-service sector would be wise to pay attention to these figures.

One of the customers we surveyed, Jared, shared a story with us about a recent visit to Jamba Juice, a quick-service retailer of better-for-you food and beverages. The service was good, but the floor was noticeably dirty. He got a tinge of the heebie-jeebies pondering if it was a reflection of how clean the food prep area was. As he was leaving he walked out the front door and spotted the manager on duty, sitting at a customer table working on his schedule while smoking a cigarette.

Jared hopped on the company website and filled out a comment form with his observations. No effort was made to recover Jared -- not even a simple thank you for taking the time to share valuable insights. What do you think the core values are of this company based on Jared's observations and the lack of response from corporate? It's fair to deduce that the manager was mirroring the organization's laissez-faire attitude.

> *74% of patrons equate restroom cleanliness with the cleanliness of a restaurant's kitchen.*
>
> *Jon Taffer, Hospitality Consultant*

If we broke this story down into its smaller parts we could train for hours on a number of subjects, so let's just focus on the root of the problem, which is staff development.

Subconsciously customers are asking themselves, if the customer area is this filthy, what's going on behind the scenes?. What does it say about their attention to detail? What does it say about their pride? Is this a reflection of my value as a customer? If you've seen even one episode of "Kitchen Nightmares," you know the answer to those questions.

# customer trigger points

Making a customer feel comfortable is about triggering the five senses of sight, smell, sound, touch and taste. So as you look at your business through the eyes of your customer, think about what they are experiencing and ask yourself, is my operation doing everything it can to create comfort? Teaching your employees how to think critically and empowering them to use good judgment is imperative as you begin to scale the business.

The retail version of the online troll. Employees act in subversive ways under the cloak of anonymity.

One of the customers from our survey happened to be in a local pub the night before we talked with her. She told us a story about how the bar staff did nothing to make her feel comfortable. She was sitting at the bar and two bartenders continued with their busywork for five minutes before they walked over and dropped down a coaster. No greeting, just eye contact. She stood up, grabbed her jacket and walked next door to another restaurant. She laughed and said it was OK, the bar top was sticky anyway.

When I was first starting my career I shared an office with a gentleman who was retired from the Hilton organization. He managed their Las Vegas property in the 1970s. He once told me that every morning he would walk the entire property with a critical eye for the details that his staff might have overlooked so that his guests would feel nothing but 100 percent comfort.

I recalled this story recently when I was standing in line at a Walgreens store. It was late February and there sat a vase of dead Valentine's flowers with a sign that read "75% OFF LAST CHANCE"

#facepalm

Oversights happen, but pride of ownership of one's job is a core value. Ensure that you're hiring properly, investing in training and inspiring your staff to contribute at their highest level.

## Seven things you can do to create a comfortable environment:

- If you are service-based, keep your vehicle clean, carry a nice portfolio, dress appropriately for your profession.
- Speak at the level of your customer. If your clients are enterprise level, then pull out your "concierge" language. Very professional and watch the humor. If you manufacture skateboards then casual is great, just make sure that you still convey professionalism, expertise and keep your eye on valuing the customer.
- Emotional comfort is extremely important when we think of Internet marketing. Immediately upon landing on a website with a company we don't know, we're making a values judgment. We are gathering data to determine if the purveyor is like us and shares our values. You have seconds to create comfort with your audience here, so work with a branding expert who can help you design a clear and concise marketing message. Show images of your staff and your facilities so that the audience begins to judge whether you share the same values.
- Brick & mortar business? A clean restroom encourages positive feelings in customers about your business. This is because customers can equate the cleanliness of your company's bathroom with the cleanliness of your entire business. This is especially true if you're a restaurant owner.

- Dust on your retail shelves? How long has the product been sitting there? It tells customers that your product line is stale. If no one else has wanted it before you, why would you want it?
- Online business? Offer free trials and money-back guarantees. When customers are buying a product or service for the first time, they want to know the business they are working with stands behind their offerings.
- Make sure that your website has your contact information prominently displayed -- consumers want to know there is someone to talk to and they don't have patience to ferret around on your site to find it.

The television show "Undercover Boss" and the use of secret shoppers have become so popular because it gives businesses an opportunity to experience their organization from a perspective they might not see otherwise. You can't fix the problems you aren't aware of. Even if you're onsite daily and you see the day-to-day operation, sometimes you're too close to it. You may not see the forest through the trees. Your customers will appreciate when you go the extra mile and implement the seven tips above.

# [10]

# "Be a Genshai"

*" Genshai is an ancient Hindi word meaning to never treat others, or yourself, in a way that makes them feel small. Lift those around you.*

The concept of "Genshai" is beautifully simple in nature. When we step out of ego and focus on serving those who have a need, everyone is elevated. There is an internal process that has to happen before your employees can effectively lift your customers. Leadership, by the simplest definition, is our ability to guide others on a desired path. Let's begin by lifting our employees with the belief that they, in turn, will lift your customers.

The main idea of "servant leadership" is that leaders serve the staff. Managers serve and treat their employees as they want those employees, in turn, to serve and treat the customers.

# leadership should be a verb

To lead is an action. Organizations make a mistake when they give people the office, position or title of leader. Every company has an organizational chart with a reporting structure that puts people in charge of certain projects, and those individuals are responsible for making sure the objectives are met. When we fail to teach these people the critical soft skills of leadership, this is when frustration, anger, confusion and ultimately an unhappy workforce is born. If you have ever worked for a technology company, you know what I'm talking about. People who know a project by way of skill and experience are put in charge of managing it and they are typically analytical thinkers and often introverts.

When you manage a project there are people involved who handle different aspects of the project. The "chosen one" is put in charge of these employees and this is where things begin to unravel from a productivity standpoint. Many analytical people have a very hard time managing others: It requires empathy, connectedness and listening to understand. They may have an underdeveloped skill level with people so they communicate poorly, they lack mentorship skills, they send mixed messages and those on the project are left feeling unfulfilled and frustrated.

There are subtleties to leadership that are Yoda-esque. They include patience, wisdom and the ability to teach through parables so that the "student," or employee in this case, connects the dots in his own mind. Even people who sew elastic on underpants in a sweatshop are thinking about how they can be more productive. The best companies to work for allow for the flow of ideas on how to improve the way it does business.

There are four different stages of development and when you match these stages with different styles of leadership, you can easily lead anyone.

# the honeymoon stage

Development stage number one is when someone is in the unknown unknowns. They don't know what they don't know. When someone first comes into a company they are mostly in this state. This is the honeymoon stage and is marked by excitement and eagerness to get started. Think back to when you were 5 or 6 years old. This is around the time we learn to ride a bike. You were probably watching your siblings or neighbors ride around with such ease. They were riding with no hands on the handlebars or coasting down a hill with their feet off the pedals. It looked so easy and effortless, didn't it?

What you didn't know then (and may not know now) is that bicycle physics is quite complex. You have to go fast in order to create stability and when you're 5, sitting on something that easily tips over when you're standing still, and being expected to create speed by pedaling in order to stabilize is counterintuitive. But regardless, what you perceive is easy is more complex when you get into it.

We match this stage of learning with a leadership style that is directive. We give step-by-step instructions on how things work. It's important that it's linear and logical so that for the employee who is thinking, "I wonder why they do it this way?" you can appropriately connect the dots in their mind.

# the deflation stage

Development stage number two is marked by frustration because what they believed looked easy from the outside is actually harder than it appears. They get frustrated and may lose confidence in their ability to get where they want to be. So going back to the bike analogy, you probably have vivid memories of falling down many times. Bloody kneecaps and tears. You didn't understand why it was so hard for you to learn. People around you were encouraging you to not give up, that you *can* learn this. In business, it's no different. We understand that systems and process take time to learn and master.

We match this stage of development with a leadership style that is first empathic -- meaning the person teaching us confirms that it's natural to feel anxious and that what you are feeling is what everyone feels at this stage. Then the leader moves back into directive mode, hits the reset button and reviews the step-by-step process from the beginning.

The employee will be hearing the instructions differently this second time around because they have a small amount of experience and are moving it from the front of the brain, where short-term storage lies, to the back of the brain where it becomes rote. So again, empathy first, then move back into directive. The employee begin to see results, gets a taste of success and confidence grows as a result.

So going back to the bike analogy, this is after you crash for the 10th time, when someone picks you up off the pavement, wipes your tears, puts a cold rag on your bloody scrape, tells you they know it hurts while they put a bandage on it, puts a magic mommy kiss on it and then encourages you to keep trying (and secretly tells you that you're much smarter than your brothers and sisters and if they can do it, you can certainly do it too).

# the high productivity stage

This is when we are comfortable and get into flow states with what we're doing. We are now riding our bike down the street, around the corner, a few blocks away to our school and perhaps just a bit further to the store. This is where we feel independence and freedom to explore the world beyond the end of our driveway.

In business, we have transitioned from apprentice to journeyman. We match this stage from a leadership perspective by creating a conduit of communication that supports a two-way conversation. It is no longer you telling an employee what to do, but rather a relationship that is based on collective problem solving and critical thinking. They are close to the work so they have a unique perspective on how to improve it so that you get better results.

The days of struggling on the bike are behind you. You're now riding with your feet on the seat working on going from crouching to standing. You're taking more risks and experimenting by getting some big air off a plywood ramp you built. You're jumping off curbs and attempting to pop a wheelie. Your friends feel confident that you know what you're doing so they hop on the handlebars and let you take them for a ride.

# the peer-to-peer stage

The final stage of development is when the employee achieves expertise. Their skill level may even surpass yours in certain areas. They are now your peer and your conversations revolve around higher-level thinking.

Even if the two of you are in different levels of an organizational chart, it should have no bearing on how you value their perspective. If you are an effective Genshai, than there is no need for fear that they will take your job. The universe is an abundant place and there is room for everyone.

Where many leaders make an error is in thinking that this individual, because you nurtured her to this stage and knew her when she knew nothing, is still beneath you and will never be at your level. This is a scarcity mindset and you should evaluate the root of that fear. A true Genshai would not harbor these thoughts. A true Genshai celebrates the success of those he lifts.

And in the dramatic conclusion of our biking parable, you're now riding side-by-side climbing the steeps of L'Alpe d'Huez in the Tour de France. You are collaborating on the strategy, you're sharing gooey carb gel packs, you're encouraging each other to push harder and dig deeper to get to the peak. He might even surprise you and break away in the final 100 feet before the finish line in a burst of energy you had never seen before. You see the look on his face and you take pride in seeing all he set out to do, and that you played some small role in elevating him in true Genshai Jedi style.

# what we need

If all else is equal, the nicer that you treat people, the more money you will earn. That is truly the bottom line. The sooner businesses accept that, the sooner they will bring in higher-grossing sales.

How do we "become" nice? According to the work of William Schutz, author of "The Interpersonal Underworld" (1966), we communicate based on three primary needs:

1. Inclusion: how we include ourselves and are included with others
2. Control: the interpersonal play of control that we exhibit over others or they exhibit over us
3. Affection: how we give and receive affection.

The first need, the need for inclusion, can be delineated by being either:

- Undersocial: The customer is ignored. This is a glaringly blatant example of how not to do business. Everything about the experience does not feel right. The customer leaves either without buying or with the understanding that he will be buying elsewhere in the future.
- Ideal: This is the perfect amount of inclusion. The customer feels acknowledged and his needs have been met. The staff was friendly. The customer felt welcomed. The entire experience within the confines of the business during that exchange was exactly how it should have been. It felt to that customer to be "just right."

- Oversocial: Have you ever been to a store and the clerk rushed over to help you? Once you mentioned that you were "just browsing," she lingered. She hung out with you the entire time you were in the store. We have all been there. It feels awkward. This is an example of oversocial or excessive inclusion. Yes, too much of a good thing isn't always a good thing.

Heralded by Fortune Magazine as the "CEO Whisperer," Anthony Robbins defines clearly six human needs, and says that if at any time three or more needs are being met, then whatever is meeting those needs can become addictive. The six needs are:

1. Connection
2. Significance
3. Certainty
4. Variety
5. Growth
6. Contribution.

Let's say for the sake of argument that his theory is true. If a business could control for three of those six needs, the customer would want to do business there every single time. Here's how your business can do just that:

- Provide certainty: Offer consistency to your guests. Ensure that every time they walk in the door they receive what they have grown accustomed to. There is something to be said for an old, soft shoe because people love knowing what to expect. This is how we manage expectations. We offer the same services/products that we are known for. We offer them at the price point we are known for. We improve our service, certainly, but we never let the experience go downhill. This is why the franchise model is so successful, because of consistency and predictability. If you go into a Chipotle in Florida it will taste like the Chipotle in Seattle.

- Provide significance: Make that customer feels like a king or a queen in your presence. Greet her by name when possible, pay attention to her and treat her as if she were your only guest.
- Provide connection: Be a Genshai. Reach him at his heart level. Kick it grandpa style. Listen to him and provide him with the level of caring that he would expect from a dear friend.

I'm sure you are curious as to what this word "Genshai" entails. As previously stated, "never treat others, or yourself, in a way that makes them feel small. Lift others up." In his TED talk, Kevin Hall describes the events surrounding the first time he heard the word Genshai. Over dinner his friend explained the Hindi word to him and offered the most beautiful example of what a Genshai's actions would be.

If you saw a man sitting on the street, begging for money, the common response would be to offer him your spare change. Maybe you would hand it to him or place it in his bucket. A friend of mine always finds the nearest sandwich shop and comes back with a sub. Hart's friend explained that a Genshai would kneel down to where the man was, look him in his eye and place the money squarely in his hand. A Genshai understands that any man could easily be in that situation and might need a hand. A Genshai recognizes his place among all men and puts himself ahead of no one. He lifts all up, including himself.

Some people feel that in order to lift others up, they must place them above where they are. We do this as parents. We oftentimes serve at the expense of our own well-being. How can you truly serve if you are shrinking?

# the way of the Genshai

A Genshai represents the ultimate in terms of respect. Respect for oneself and respect for others. In order to be a Genshai, one must be able to visualize all situations in this manner in order to properly lift all.

- Step one. Visualize looking down at the customer in your care. This does NOT mean that you are looking down on a person or treating her disrespectfully. Remember, this is not from Western culture. Stretch your mind in a different direction. The downward glance is simply an understanding that she has come to you to be lifted. That is all.
- Step two. Meet her exactly where she is.. Think about Schutz's work. Try to match and mirror your customer's communication needs through active listening and creating the customer experience. If you serve her properly and you pay attention to her cues and interpersonal communication needs, she will guide you to create the ultimate customer experience.
- Step three. Visualize lifting up the guest. This will be accomplished through three different modes.

- First, follow the Golden Rule. All situations can be made better through kindness.
- Secondly, ask questions and offer her appropriate information and knowledge to help guide her decisions.
- Third, your ultimate objective is to make her day better. We have offered statistics throughout this book related to how a customer feels and how that connects with her purchasing habits. This isn't about what she bought, it is about how the transaction made her feel. If you actually make someone's day better, she will always come back to you. Let Matt from Stagecoach Coffee serve as your model.

Now you know what a Genshai is, how to achieve it through your actions and the importance of it as it relates to the bottom line of your business. If you want your business to become "addictive" to your customer to the point where he always keeps you top-of-mind, remember to provide certainty, significance and connection. Be that Genshai and you will always make that interpersonal connection.

# [11]

# "Respect My Money"

*"I believe in the flow of energy in money, so instead of handing back my change all at once, kindly count it out. My money is like gold."*

ONE OF THE MOST beautiful pieces of prose I have stumbled on that expresses how money was valued in our grandparents' age -- really the age before credit cards, was captured in an autobiographical novel, *Through A Portagee Gate*, by Charles Reis Felix.

The time was the 1940s and it was the night before Charlie left for college at the University of Michigan. The son of Portuguese immigrants, his father sat him down so that he could give him money for his first semester of school.

The author writes,

> "He took a rubber band off the roll. He started counting it out. It was slow going. The bills were all curled up. He had to try and straighten them out. He wanted to make sure there weren't two bills stuck together. So as he counted he rubbed each bill with his thumb and forefinger. He counted in Portu-

guese murmuring each number. He put the bills in the stack. When he got to $100 in his count, he started a new stack.

The bills were mostly fives, some 2's some 1's, a few 10's, but absolutely no $20's.

The bills were like the people they had come from. Shabby, ill used, worn out, grimy, wrinkled with the corners gone. There wasn't a clean crisp middle class bill in the bunch. I felt a strong emotion watching him count. I knew what this money meant to him. He had accumulated it slowly. One bill at a time. How many little ten-cent jobs, a strap falling off, a tongue needing re-sewing did this money represent. Its growth had been fertilized by his sweat. When he finished, the roll had come out to exactly four stacks of $100 each.

'Now you count it Charlie. Make sure it's all there. Take your time. If there's a mistake, now is the time to find it.'

I counted out loud in English. He watched me closely. I counted slowly. To have counted rapidly or casually would have shown disrespect for the moment, and would have disparaged him."

When we physically hand money over to a business in exchange for a product or service, what the transaction actually represents is the time it took to earn it. Most people exchange time for dollars. Time away from their family, friends and hobbies -- all the things they care about and value.

To have the recipient of that money dismiss it by not thoughtfully appreciating that without this flow of income, the business would not exist is inexcusable. How many times during the day do we transact with businesses who do not express appreciation when the exchange happens? Even the simple act of counting back change is a thing of the past. Change is rarely counted back. Occasionally the amount is read from the register, but most often it is handed back in one handful and is devoid of a proper thank you.

What customers desire is the recognition and thanks from businesses that there are other choices and our choice to work with them should be valued. The exchange of money is the final point in the transaction. How a customer feels when they walk out the door should boil down to one idea:

**That the customer is confident their money was spent at the right business.**

Recently I switched contracts for cellular over to Verizon Wireless. I was a little unhappy after I saw my first bill. There were some unanticipated charges on there. So I went back to speak with a manager. I was very controlled, but I was visibly upset. I felt like there was some bait and switch happening. But, the point of me sharing this case study with you is to share with you the response from the manager, which was really right on point. He did exactly what I'm teaching you to do in this training. I couldn't walk away angry because I was so proud of the way in which he managed me. What this manager did really effectively, even though I did not get my desired outcomes, was in the questions he asked and how actively he listened to understand me. The way he treated me in the process of solving my complaint honored my value as a customer.

> *"When customers share their story with you, they're not just sharing pain points. They're actually teaching you how to make your product, service, and business better."*
>
> *Kristin Smaby, Being Human is Good Business*

What this means is that you have to create an environment where your customers feel open to share feedback and have the mindset that this feedback is designed to help you improve the way you do business.

*78% of consumers have bailed on a transaction or not made an intended purchase because of a poor customer experience.*

*Lee Resources*

Seventy-eight percent have bailed on a transaction! That is serious money being lost! So, here is a reasonable deduction. An abandoned cart is less likely to happen if you're providing an exceptional experience.

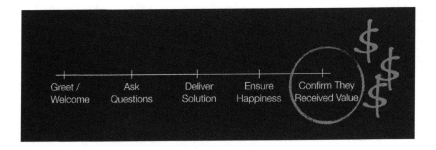

The perfect transaction (from left to right) starts with the greeting and the welcome. We ask diagnostic questions to understand what is it that the customer wants, needs or desires. We match them with our solution. We deliver that solution. We ensure that this is exactly what they are looking for. Then we confirm that they have received value.

The end point is where the big money lies when you get this exactly right. If they are 100 percent satisfied they'll perpetuate word of mouth marketing and bring referrals to you, right? If it's not 100 percent to their satisfaction, then you risk lost income in the form of not just that individual customer, but the compounded effect of the negative word of mouth.

We all know that it's much more expensive to acquire a new customer than it is to retain an existing one.

In the process of resolving a conflict you need to understand this key number: the lifetime value of your customer. Where owners make the biggest mistake is that they're focusing on the cost of resolving the conflict without regard for the lifetime value of the customer.

## When you do have conflict with a customer, your goals are two-fold:

1. To resolve the customer's concern
2. To ask whether there is a lesson to take forward that will help you improve the way you do business.

How is customer recovery used to improve your retention and why is listening so critical to that process?

Let's begin by examining the root of what is inarguably the cause of every source of anger, frustration, disappointment that customers feel when the transaction goes off the rails. The root cause of all of these emotions is *unmet expectations*. What we can do is manage expectations and recover the customer when those expectations are not met.

Let's begin with understanding the meaning and the power of customer recovery. This is a term that's used in the hospitality industry for when a guest is dissatisfied and how the staff is trained to respond so that they'll be happy enough with the resolution that they'll come back and continue to refer others. It's an extremely delicate little process and it requires you and your staff to put your best foot forward and keep your eye on the goal.

Ritz Carlton empowers its employees to spend up to $2,000 to solve guests' problems without asking for a manager's approval. This has gotten a lot of ink in the press because everybody was blown away by this number. That seems like a lot of money to resolve a customer issue, doesn't it? Why would they do that?

It's actually not a lot of money when you consider that the lifetime value of a Ritz-Carlton guest is $250,000. So $2,000 is less than 1 percent of the lifetime value. The Ritz-Carlton wants to empower their staff to create a resolution very, very quickly. When you think about their ideal customer, it makes perfect sense. These are high net worth individuals, they are highly influential, they are used to getting what they want quickly, they are highly demanding and don't care about excuses, they only care about results. Besides, they could cause you a lot of pain with one tweet.

On this note, the influence people have on social networks determines the speed with which many enterprise-level companies react to recover them and the degree to which they will bend in order to not have their reputation affected online.

A friend of mine who has a massive Twitter following was bumped from her United flight and automatically put on one the following day. She could not get resolution using the customer service phone number, so she tweeted about her discontent. United was tracking the social airwaves, picked up her tweet, saw that she had a very high Klout score (a way of tracking reach and influence across Facebook, Twitter, LinkedIn and other social media) and immediately accommodated her request.

So influence is flexed not just offline through word of mouth, but also online. Except online it is immediate and permanent.

So as this relates to your business, the key points that you want to base recovery decisions on are simple: the lifetime value of your customer and the social influence of the customer. For local businesses, just one transaction gone awry with one influential person could hurt sales. Imagine that they have one thousand followers locally. If they hop on Facebook to say the pizza they received from a specific pizza joint was delivered two hours after it was ordered, it could do irreparable harm to the business' reputation.

> *A typical business hears from 4% of its dissatisfied customers. Only 4%!*
>
> Ruby Newell-Legner, Understanding Customers

Ninety-six out of 100 people who are unhappy are saying nothing. Nada, zilch, zippo. This is money that's leaking out of your business. The best way to let these 96 percent of the dissatisfied customers know that you care about their opinion is to ask them for constructive feedback on a consistent basis.

Now, for the 4 percent who do take the time to give you feedback in the form of a complaint, they need to be treated in a very specific way so you recover them. They can do massive damage to your reputation both offline in the form of word-of-mouth marketing and online through ratings and review sites if unresolved. So take every reasonable action to retain them.

# Here are some high-level things to keep in mind as you're 'making the situation right' for your customer:

- Most customers understand that things will and can go wrong. What they don't understand, accept or find interesting are excuses.
- Do not panic. With most customers and in most situations, customers' sense of trust and camaraderie *increases* after a problem is successfully resolved. It actually builds loyalty when resolved in their favor.
- Avoid assuming you know what solution a customer wants or "should" want. Ask.
- Don't strive for "fairness" or "justice." Creating or preserving a customer's warm feelings for a company isn't about fairness or justice. It's about being treated especially well.
- Don't imagine you're doing something special for a customer by making things how they should have been in the first place.

## 11 Steps to Customer Recovery

## STEP 1: INTRODUCE YOURSELF

This is oftentimes overlooked. Oftentimes we walk up to them and we just say, "How may I help you?" instead of introducing yourself. For example, "Hi. My name is Pamela. I'm the manager of this store. How may I assist you?" Extend your hand. Be sure to tell them your title.

## STEP 2: LET THEM TALK

This is their opportunity to vent and just get everything off their chest. Be prepared that this may go on for a bit. Be patient. Don't react or respond until they are done. Interrupting is a major no-no as it sends a variety of different messages like:

- "I'm not listening because I'm busy thinking about my response."
- "I'm more important than you are."
- "What I have to say is more interesting, accurate, or relevant."
- "I don't really care what you think."
- "I don't have time for your opinion."
- "This isn't a conversation, it's a contest, and I'm going to win."

## STEP 3: BE PRESENT

Maintain eye contact and mentally screen out distractions, like background activity and noise. Apologize if something does create a distraction so that the customer feels like your No.1 priority in that moment.

## STEP 4: LISTEN WITHOUT JUMPING TO CONCLUSIONS

This requires you to slow down your thought process. This is a skill, and it can be developed over time with practice. Remember that the speaker is using language to represent the thoughts and feelings inside their brain. So, picture what they're saying. Allow your mind to create a mental model of the information being communicated. So whether it's a literal picture, or an arrangement of abstract concepts, your brain will do the necessary work if you stay focused and keep your senses fully alert. When listening for long stretches, concentrate on and remember key words and phrases, especially emotionally based ones. When it's your turn to listen, don't spend the time planning what to say next. You can't rehearse and listen at the same time. Think only about what the other person is saying.

## STEP 5: BODY LANGUAGE

Maintain an open body stance. Nod to show your understanding through appropriate facial expressions and an occasional well-timed "hmmm" or "uh huh." Face to face with a person, you can detect enthusiasm, boredom or irritation very quickly with the expression around the eyes, the set of the mouth and the slope of the shoulders. These are clues you can't ignore. When listening, remember that words convey only a fraction of the message.

## STEP 6: YOUR RESPONSE

Begin your response with a thank you. Express gratitude to them for bringing this to your attention, because really this valuable feedback helps your company improve the way you do business. For example, "First of all, I sincerely appreciate you bringing this to my attention. We rely on customers like you to share your experiences so that we can take the proper steps to ensure another customer doesn't have to go through what you're going through." That would be an appropriate "thank you" so that they understand the importance of the conversation.

## STEP 7: MANAGE THEIR EXPECTATIONS

Assure them that their expectations were not unwarranted and that they have every right to feel the way they do. Really identify with their feelings. For example, "I'm so sorry. I can totally relate to your frustration and that should have never happened."

## STEP 8: ASK CLARIFYING QUESTIONS

Clarifying questions helps solidify the key issues, so make sure you understand exactly what the person is saying and what they want.

## STEP 9: YOUR MAGIC WAND

This is the secret sauce right here. You may have a lot of ideas at this point in the conversation as to how to resolve their problem, and maybe it's easy enough to just take care of them, in which case you should. Or, perhaps you're totally unclear as to what they want, which happens when somebody goes on a tirade. Here is a way to get to the bottom line,

*"If I could wave my magic wand to make this situation right for you so that you leave 100% happy, what would that take?"*

This is exactly the phrasing that the manager at Verizon used with me. He whipped out the magic wand trick and I was so impressed because this is exactly what you want to do. If you're overwhelmed and you're not tracking exactly what the problem is and what resolution they want, pull out your magic wand and ask them.

This lets you start the solution phase with the end in mind. You know what is important to them and what they value the most. Don't guess. Be sure to ask. Their answer is going to be the destination you want to put the conversation on the path toward.

## STEP 10: REVERSE-ENGINEER THE SOLUTION

You've asked them what they want in order to leave 100 percent satisfied. Now deliver it if it's reasonable and doable. But let's say the thing they want is impossible for you to deliver. Let your core values be your compass. Think about the lifetime value of your customer and what's at stake. Let this guide your solutions with the objective of recovery. Remember, they are going to talk about this so ensure they are telling the story about how fantastic you were at resolving the problem.

## STEP 11: FOLLOW UP

This is another tactic that few businesses use, but has enormous long-term value for building loyalty. Drop a handwritten card in the mail expressing how important your business is to you. Throwing in a gift card for even the smallest amount demonstrates more about your core values than the value of the card. Customers love this!

Let's take a moment to address how we handle those extreme customers who are thankfully few and far between (1-2 percent of all customers), and are unreasonable, unrealistic and inconsolable. When their expectations are unmet and your efforts to resolve their complaint is not successfully recovering the customer, then you will want some reasonable approaches as to how to manage this. The thing we have to understand and accept is that this is how these people live their life all day, every day. Once you've done everything you possibly can, unless you're a jackass whisperer, your job is to get out of this situation as tactfully as possible.

There is specific language that keeps you in control as you stay professional and maintain your boundaries. Keep a positive spin on your communication. So for example: "We sincerely appreciate that you have given us the opportunity to resolve this situation to your liking. This is what we're able to do for you ..." Do you hear the boundary in this? You're saying, "This is what we're able to do." Avoid phrases such as, "We can't do that ..." "I don't know ..." or "No." That's just going to incite more fury.

If it's in accordance with your core values, be prepared to let this customer go. This is your business and you get to decide whom you want to work with. If a customer's values are out of alignment with yours, then there isn't anything you can do to change that. Just stay very proactive. Maintain your boundaries. Let them know that you sincerely appreciate their feedback and the opportunity to make the situation right, and then tell them what you are able to do for them.

Depending on your business, you can take a pre-emptive approach to *avoid* customer dissatisfaction.

So think about how you can stand out by doing little things to provide massive value to your customers and demonstrate that you're respecting your customer's money by providing awesome value. Use my mother's floral shop and the old Portuguese shoe repairman as your guide as you reconnect with the value of your customers' contribution to the success of your company.

# [12]

# "Dazzle Me"

*Wow me! The chord of appreciation has been lying dormant within my emotional fabric."*

IT SERVES US TO reflect on the way business was conducted in past generations because the old-fashioned way is still the essence of localism, scrappy entrepreneurship and developing relationships.

Businesses that are best positioned to thrive in today's economy are returning to the simple practice of quality conversations that were the hallmarks of building and maintaining an enterprise back in the day. Even 50 years ago, all aspects of life moved at a slower pace. Given the limitations of technology, the speed of communication was often restricted to how fast the information was passed over the neighbor's fence or on the telephone. The effect this had on personal and business relationships was profound -- there was time to deliberately develop relationships on a deeper level.

What was the secret behind Mom & Pop's business success? The advantages haven't changed in all these years. They were and still are rooted in providing unique products, exceptional service and a highly personalized buying experience. They made the treatment of their customers a number one priority because the survival of their business depended on getting and keeping customers.

They did what comes naturally and organically; they developed rapport, which over time led to a trusting relationship that fueled repeat business. What this translates to in terms of customer experience was so simple and yet so purposeful in making customers feel valued.

*Kick it old school*

## They connected in these ways:

- A proper greeting with a sincere smile. "Welcome! What brings you in today?" Customers came through the door looking for something the business had to offer -- a solution.

Business owners recognized this and showed their gratitude.

- A simple acknowledgement of your presence. If they were
serving another customer they took a moment to look up
and thank you in advance for your patience." I'll be right
with you."

- An ability to gain the understanding of what was most important to the customer, what they cared most about and
valued. They asked the right questions in order to find the
right solution.

- The entire buying experience was about being creative and
thinking of purposeful up-sells that took the solution to the
next level. When employees asked questions, it was with
the intention of learning more about the customer, so the
customer felt heard.

- Offered a sincere gesture of gratitude for coming into the
store, regardless of whether it resulted in a transaction.

> *"We are superior to the competition because we hire employees who work in an environment of belonging and purpose. We foster a climate where the employee can deliver what the customer wants. You cannot deliver what the customer wants by controlling the employee."*
>
> *Horst Schulze, Former Ritz Carlton President*

## Be unexpectedly quirky

Have you ever taken the time to read those lengthy smartphone
update agreements for your apps before you mindlessly click "I
agree"? The team at Camera+, through the magic of the written
word, has pulled back the proverbial curtain for us to see what the

elusive world of an app developer looks like. Granted, no one (OK, maybe one person) reads these update announcements, but this is a great example of how a business delivers messages to their customers with courtesy and personality.

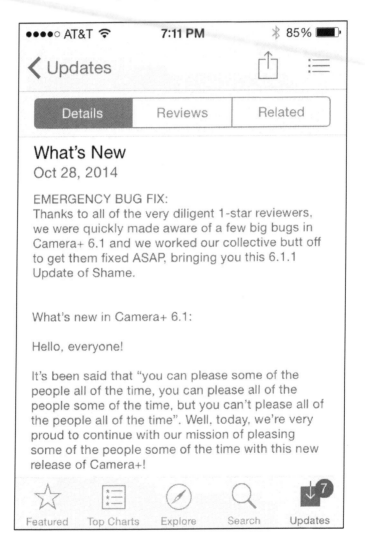

With technology, you have no choice but to listen to your customer feedback and make adjustments. Your success is hinging on a positive user experience. Here is where customer ratings and reviews play another important role in how a business meets its market.

Our expectation is that everything is going to be perfect every time. What Camera+ does well here is humorously tell us they are listening to those reviews and that they are working toward exceeding those expectations and are making adaptations in how they deliver their solution.

These are just some of the things that successful business can do today to set themselves apart. By doing this they are uniquely positioned to stand out in our struggling economy. Those businesses that are willing and able to implement this sense of connectedness will see massive growth in their revenue.

To keep your finger on the pulse of your connectedness with your customers and know how to dazzle them:

## It boils down to one simple question

*On a scale between 1 and 10, how likely is it that you would recommend our company/products/service to a friend or colleague?*

A tool to measure customer satisfaction that many enterprise level companies use is called a Net Promoter Score (NPS®). By asking the one simple question above, businesses can make improvements that result in customer loyalty and grow their profits. Depending on how customers respond to the question, they are categorized as either Promoters, Detractors or Passives.

- Promoters (score 9-10) are loyal enthusiasts who will keep buying and refer others, fueling growth.
- Passives (score 7-8) are satisfied but unenthusiastic customers who are vulnerable to competitive offerings.
- Detractors (score 0-6) are unhappy customers who can damage your brand and impede growth through negative word-of-mouth.

*"We're living in what I like to call the 'Thank You Economy,' because only the companies that can figure out how to mind their manners in a very old-fashioned way -- and do it authentically -- are going to have a prayer of competing."*

*Gary Vaynerchuk, Author "The Thank You Economy"*

Enterprise-level companies use this tool to identify trends on a high level and make adjustments. For example, at JetBlue, they may hear from a respondent that he gave them a score of 7 because the wait at Portland Airport ticket counter was too long. As JetBlue aggregates and tracks this feedback they can see if it's a one-off complaint or if it is a widely held concern, in which case they would weigh how to make operational changes to satisfy the concern.

## The Main Street Advantage

Small businesses can use this type of information through your own informal research. Proactively requesting feedback is a way to see your business through your customer's eyes. Create a survey card asking just one question: "On a scale between 1 and 10, how likely are you to refer others to my business?" You can distribute a survey to your customers right after they leave by emailing them a link to a survey. To get started with surveys, we highly recommend www.surveymonkey.com or Forms in Google Drive.

Take a page from the Net Promoter model, but instead of having three tiers of respondents, throw it into the framework of "pass" or "fail," with anything less than an 8 being a fail. Why? Because if a customer is neutral on your business then that means they are the equivalent of a free agent. They don't have loyalty to your brand and are vulnerable to your competitor's offerings.

The low-hanging fruit is to hit the Passives hard with some sweet, sweet love in order to demonstrate that you value them. This is the way to graduate them from Passive to Promoter so that they are talking about your business in a positive way.

The ultimate test for any customer experience initiative is whether it helps the business grow sales. The value is that it helps you and your employees clarify and simplify the job of creating an exceptional customer experience.

# [13]

# "Thank Me"

*"When you look me in the eye, smile and sincerely thank me for my business, it connects me to you and your brand. The purpose of business is to get and keep customers, so show me sincere appreciation for my business."*

Let every day be Thanksgiving Day. Hearing the words of thanks has a nice ring to it, but nothing is more gratifying than a gesture of thanks. Every business is in the customer experience business, so strive to continually demonstrate your thanks to your customers.

## Here are 16 ways to express gratitude:

The very smart people at HelpScout.com came up with this fabulous list of ways to express gratitude.
- Look your customer in the eye and hand her credit card back with two hands. It shows you're honoring her.

- Model Nordstrom and walk around the counter and thank your customer when you hand him his bag.
- A handwritten note of thanks. Make it specific and personal. It doesn't have to be long. Remember it's the gesture. It just feels good to get this in the mail, doesn't it?
- Help customers learn something new. This is where email marketing comes in handy. Always be providing value. Share articles and videos that are fun, funny, educational and interesting.
- Come up front and spend time with your customers. You'll learn about your business through their eyes. Show gratitude for the information.
- Give the gift of a good read. There isn't anyone who doesn't appreciate the thought of a book. Be sure to write a personal message on the inside so they know it was picked out just for them.
- Reward social media engagement. This is hugely valuable to your customers. You could set up an informal points structure and track who likes, comments and shares your content. Once you get into paid advertising through Facebook (which is the most powerful way to advertise today) you will understand the pure value of the engagement of your perfect customer. It's gold!
- Buy a distant customer a cup of coffee, just because. Send her a gift card and a note to let her know you're thinking of her.
- Spotlight customers on your website. Testimonials -- especially above the fold of your home page -- are proven converting strategies for that critical social proof.

- Send a sweet treat. We love the Christie Cookies Company. They're delivered in a tin and taste like heaven.
- Give a charitable gift in their honor.
- Send cards on unique holidays. Groundhogs Day. Half-birthday. International Talk Like a Pirates Day. Have fun and get silly.
- Discount their bill, just because. A restaurant did that for my table of six girlfriends after we told the waiter we were celebrating 25 years of friendship.
- Give some swag. Who doesn't love a koozie?
- Ring the bell. Kick it Arby's style and put a bell by your door so that customers can signal to other customers and employees that they had a good experience.
- Give a big loud thanks. When you walk into Big Bill's NY Pizza in Centennial, Colo., to pick up your to-go order and leave a tip, the cashier yells over his shoulder to the cooks, "Pamela just gave us a tip." To which all the cooks yell back in unison,

# "Thanks for the tip, Pamela!"

# [13]

# Conclusion

IN TODAY'S HIGH-TECH and digital communication age, we are bombarded every day, both personally and professionally, with a virtual chaos of information. We live in a culture of live-streaming and short-term gratification. We have had more information hurtling toward us in the last 10 years than in all of history combined, and as a result the scales have been tipped in the way we communicate.

Our relationships are being nurtured through texting, email, instant messaging and social media. These bursts and snippets alter the ways we communicate. We are interacting differently and as a result, less emphasis is placed on developing the skills required for healthy interpersonal relationships.

## Networked but further apart

Sociologists tell us that people are starved for attention these days. Despite the fact that we're more "connected" than ever, folks are hungry for face-to-face interactions and someone to really, sincerely listen to them. Consumers today are more educated about how they are being marketed to and they are attuned to who in business is actually listening to them. Those individuals and businesses that are investing their time in truly listening are developing relationships more quickly, and with relationships come lasting loyalty.

Like Disney, you should focus on improving your experiences by improving your processes. The bigger your business gets, the more important systems and process become. Always keep improving.

# the next generation

While this book is intended to educate and inform businesses about growth strategies, we are as much about consumer advocacy. As more consumers become aware of how they can help support a business they love, or warn other consumers about a business that isn't worthy of spending money on, well, this is where business will feel the pressure to meet the market at the new high-water mark.

While visiting my daughter at college in Chicago, we were going in and out of stores in the Wicker Park neighborhood. As soon as we walked out the door of a shop she was giving me her opinion on the customer experience. It was great to see how her worldview on the customer experience has changed -- especially after working for a few months for Starbucks before she started college.

Even my parents are seeing their role as consumers differently. They recently told me that they switched their credit card to Jet-Blue even though they could get better rates with another card.

When I asked why they said that since they are frequent fliers on that airline and the employees are always so nice and helpful. They wanted to spend their money with companies they liked.

The Internet is changing faster than we can possibly imagine. It is a tool that can absolutely drive traffic to your business. What is working today with Internet marketing might not work in six months. What will never change, however, is our desire to feel valued. I've provided you with the blueprint on how to implement a few key strategies and now, like every decision in your business, the rest is up to you to decide how you want to proceed. Yes or no. No longer can you sit on the fence hoping for divine intervention. Take swift action and put these proven concepts into play.

# [15]

# Ready. Aim. Fire.

Check out this list of all the steps you want to take as you design and implement an exceptional customer experience for your business:

1.  Put your consumer hat on and ask yourself this question, "What does a business have to do in order to earn your loyalty?"
2.  What makes your business different from your competition when it comes to the customer experience?
3.  Are you willing to continually strive to improve so that you are always the best in your category?
4.  Are you open to the idea that there is always room for improvement in the way you deliver an exceptional customer experience?
5.  What are your business's core values and how do you currently ensure that they are being perceived at every level of your business?

6. If core values are already in place in your business, what level of participation did your employees play in the creation of them?

7. Identify core values.

    a. Yours

    b. Your staff's

    c. Combine them to design 10 company core values

8. On a scale between 1 and 10, how competent are you in the following skill areas:

    a. SEO

    b. Social Media

    c. Local Search

    d. Video Marketing

    e. Paid Advertising

9. If you gave yourself a score less than 5 in any of these areas, you will want to develop competency by investing in your education. I highly recommend *The 5 Pillars to Online Marketing* at www.TheCustomerManifesto.com/5Pillars -- Use the coupon code: TCM and get $50 off.

10. Make sure your website is mobile responsive.

11. Have your web developer make your phone number a click through for mobile access.

12. Monitor your online reputation.

13. Set up your business in local online directories like YellowPages.com, TripAdvisor, Google+, etc.

14. Engage with your customers in social media.

15. Post content in social media consistently (2-3 times per day) with content of value to your targeted audience.

16. Answer the following questions:

    a. How are my customers greeted when they call my business, come to my store, or immediately upon landing on my website.

    b. In your processes now, how do you lead a customer from the 'hello' to rapport and relationship?

    c. What is the one-time transaction value of your customer?

    d. What is the lifetime value of your customer?

17. Can your greeting be modified to match the intention of your customer? (Are they coming in to browse or typically come in for a specific solution).

*18.* Put a date on the calendar to train your employees on the *Five Components To Making Someone Feel Welcome.*

19. With your staff identify where your customers typically need help and create actions and language around how you're going to meet and exceed those anticipated needs.

20. Review the *Barriers To Effective Listening* [page 37].

21. Review *The 9 Things You Can Do To Become a Better Listener* [page 41].

22. Create a language of service around your core values specific to the needs of your customer with the goal of delivering it on an exceptional level.

23. Deliver a customer 'experience.'

24. Identify your pickle.

25. Conduct a physical walk-through of your business looking at it as if you were your customer.

26. Is it clean, dusted, odor free, and tidy? (Would the 5-second rule apply? In other words, if your second baby dropped their pacifier on the floor would you give it a cur-

sory wipe off and put it back in their mouth, or would you have to boil it?).

27. Review the 7 things you can do to create a comfortable environment for your customers [page 63].

28. Invest in developing leadership skills.

29. Ensure that you are conveying to your customer that their money is valued.

30. Review the 11 Steps For Customer Recovery [page 84].

31. Create a process for handling unhappy customers.

32. Train your employees on the recovery process.

33. Survey your customers, "On a scale between 1-10 how likely are you to recommend my company/product/ service to your friend or colleague?"

34. With every transaction, ask your customer if you've successfully delivered a 5-star experience. Give them a card with two pieces of information: The URL to a review website like Google+ and the phone number of the owner so that if it's not a 5-star experience, they have direct contact with the person in charge.

35. Develop a plan to survey your customers with a pass or fail grade.

36. Implement strategies that address the feedback to raise this grade.

37. Review the 16 ways to express gratitude [page 99] and identify 5 that you can bring into your business today.

38. Train your staff to perfect the thank you and deliver it in a way that shows sincere gratitude for the sale.

ABOUT THE AUTHOR

With over 20 years experience in B2C as a small business consultant, New Media marketer, speaker and best-selling author, Pamela Herrmann's mission is to bring best practices from top companies that excel at creating an exceptional customer experience to the hard-working people who own local businesses. She is the founder of the website Reach Across The Register. Pamela resides in Colorado with her two children.

52095559R00067

Made in the USA
Charleston, SC
10 February 2016